TERRY FOX
and me

Dear Thomas
This is a STORY of Friendship
Courage
Kindness
Compassion and
Determination . . . .
qualiTies which we proudly see
in you !!!
You are an exceptional boy!
Love
Meymah

I will never forget how you leaned
up to help Terry with his
race. You are a
CHAMPion
Burlym

FOR DOUG AND TERRY

With great thanks to the Fox family, Rick Hansen and
my believers Jeff, Djina and Liz K. — MBL

For my son Leo, whose sportsmanship never ceases to amaze me — MP

TEXT COPYRIGHT © 2020 BY MARY BETH LEATHERDALE
ILLUSTRATIONS COPYRIGHT © 2020 BY MILAN PAVLOVIĆ

Tundra Books, an imprint of Penguin Random House Canada Young Readers,
a Penguin Random House Company

LIBRARY AND ARCHIVES CANADA CATALOGUING IN PUBLICATION

Title: Terry Fox and me / written by Mary Beth Leatherdale ; illustrated by Milan Pavlović.
Names: Leatherdale, Mary Beth, author. | Pavlović, Milan (Illustrator), illustrator.
Identifiers: Canadiana (print) 20200151983 | Canadiana (ebook) 20200152009
ISBN 9780735267688 (hardcover) | ISBN 9780735267695 (EPUB)
Subjects: LCSH: Fox, Terry, 1958-1981—Childhood and youth—Juvenile literature.
LCSH: Cancer—Patients—Biography—Juvenile literature.
LCSH: Runners (Sports)—Canada—Biography—Juvenile literature.
Classification: LCC RC265.6.F68 L43 2020 | DDC j362.196/9940092—dc23
Issued in print and electronic formats.

Published simultaneously in the United States by Tundra Books of Northern New York,
an imprint of Penguin Random House Canada Young Readers, a Penguin Random House Company

LIBRARY OF CONGRESS CONTROL NUMBER: 2019955890

Edited by Elizabeth Kribs
Designed by John Martz
The illustrations in this book were created with pencils, crayons and inks.
The text was set in Iowan Old Style.

PRINTED AND BOUND IN CHINA

www.penguinrandomhouse.ca

2 3 4 5   24 23 22 21 20

Penguin
Random House
tundra | TUNDRA BOOKS

TERRY FOX
and me

written by MARY BETH LEATHERDALE

illustrated by MILAN PAVLOVIĆ

tundra

EVERY FRIENDSHIP STARTS SOMEWHERE. Ours begins at the Mary Hill Cobras basketball tryouts in a small city in British Columbia, where two rivers meet and become one.

The coach blows his whistle and the drills begin. The kid in the yellow shirt is the only one shorter than me. *What if I'm the worst player?* I dribble. I pass. I shoot baskets. I block shots. I make the first string!

The short kid *is* the worst player. His name is Terry Fox. The coach says wrestling might be a better sport for him. But if Terry comes to practice, the coach won't cut him from the team. I shouldn't be glad that I'm better than Terry . . . but I am.

The next day, the phone rings. It's Terry.

"Hi, Doug. Want to play some one-on-one?
I need to work on my game."

"Naw, I can't. I'm busy," I say. I'm not really busy. I just
don't want to play with the worst kid on the team.

A week later, Terry's still calling. This guy won't give up.
And I like to win. So I say yes.

School ends but all summer long, Terry and I practise. Terry learns to keep his head up. Stay low. Step back. Fake.

Terry's not so bad. He's funny. He likes science. Best of all, he loves basketball, too. Even though I beat him every game, he never complains.

By the time school starts, Terry is good enough to be on the roster. One of the twelve best players on the team. And I have a new best friend.

Before long, we're in high school. Terry grows taller than me. Now, when we play one-on-one, he beats me 21–0. I don't mind losing to Terry, though. (Well, only a little.)

Terry and I don't hang out much anymore. He's busy with his new basketball teammates. Going to parties. And hanging out with friends.

I'm busy, too. Training for the biggest cross-country race of my life — the provincial championships.

Cross-country is the one sport Terry doesn't like. Maybe it's because he's always far behind me.

The night before the championship, my mind is spinning.
What if I start too fast and lose steam by the end?
Or I hang back too long? What if I'm the slowest runner?

Brrring. Brrring. The phone startles me. It's Terry.
"Good luck tomorrow," he says. "Just do your best,
Doug. One step at a time."

All through the race, Terry's voice echoes in my head.
I win the second-place medal!

When university starts, Terry and I drive to the campus in his old, beat-up car. Over the rattle of the muffler, he tells me his knee is hurting — probably from basketball practice on the hard gym floor. He doesn't want the coach to know.

But a few weeks later, Terry can barely walk. So he goes to the hospital.

When I visit Terry the next day, I see tears rolling down his face. He has a rare type of cancer. They're going to amputate his leg!

Terry is the best athlete that I know.
What can he do with only one leg?

But Terry says not to feel sorry for him. Losing his leg
is just a new challenge. After his operation, he shows
me a magazine article about a guy with one leg who
ran the New York City Marathon.

"Maybe I'll run across Canada," he says.

I believe him.

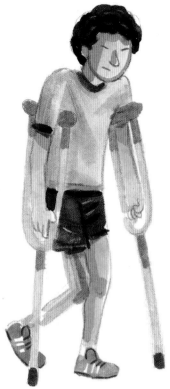

Terry stays at the hospital while he learns to walk with his prosthesis. He looks like the Bionic Man — all fibreglass and steel where the rest of his leg used to be.

At first, Terry practises walking with two crutches.

Then one crutch.

Then just a cane.

One day, when I'm bringing him some schoolwork, he surprises me at the elevator, empty hands raised in victory.

"How'd you walk here?" I ask.

"One step at a time," he says with a grin.

The months speed by with treatments at the cancer clinic.

As soon as Terry is finished with the treatments, he starts weight training to build his strength. Playing wheelchair basketball helps, too.

Sometimes we race up the pine tree–covered mountain — Terry in his wheelchair and me on foot. I always give him a head start. He says hearing my footsteps behind him makes him push harder. Seeing Terry in front of me makes me push harder, too.

Terry tells me a secret: He wants to run across Canada to raise money for cancer research.

"Will you help me train?"

I tell him to start slow. Run a little farther each day. Give his body time to recover. In a year or two, he'll be ready.

But it's not just Terry's body that has to adapt to running. His artificial leg does, too. Terry and his prosthetist — a person who makes artificial limbs — get to work.

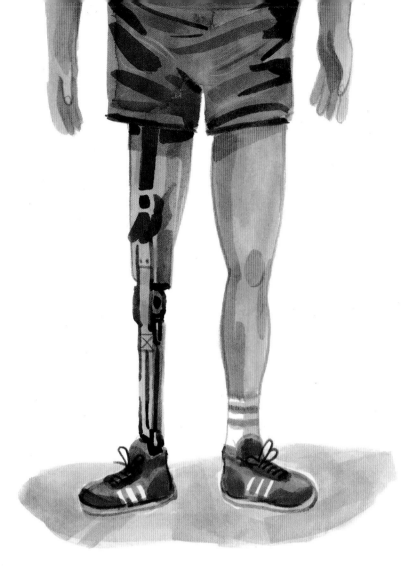

They start with a regular artificial leg for walking:
Fibreglass bucket. Metal shaft. Springs. Gears. Foot made
of wood and rubber.

They add special parts for running: Steel hinge for the knee.
Belt to attach the leg. Elastic strap to pull the leg forward.

Still, the heavy artificial leg moves too slowly. So Terry adjusts
his gait: two steps with his good leg while his artificial leg
swings forward.

Even with the new leg, running is very painful
for Terry. But that doesn't stop him.

Terry runs at night under the warm glow
of the stars. Some nights, I run with him.
Some nights, he runs by himself.

Hop, hop on his left leg.
Long step with his right.

By the end of the summer, Terry is running 8 kilometres a day. I ask him if he wants to enter a race with me.

When he tells me to enter him in the shorter distance, I push him. "You run almost that far now. Why don't you run the longer distance? It will be a bigger challenge."

For a few minutes, Terry doesn't say a word. Then he answers.

"Ok, Doug. I'll do it!"

The 28-kilometre race is gruelling. The course is steep and along a busy highway. I finish eighth — one of my best times. Terry comes in last, grinning from ear to ear.

The crowd cheers.

"That's my best friend!" I shout.
(If it's the truth, it's not really bragging.)

We begin planning for Terry's cross-country run. He'll start in St. John's, Newfoundland, next spring. To make it back home to British Columbia before winter, Terry will have to run a marathon every day — two hundred marathons in a row. No one else in the world has ever run that far on one leg.

1. ST. JOHN'S, NEWFOUNDLAND, 2. DARTMOUTH, NOVA SCOTIA,
3. CHARLOTTETOWN, PRINCE EDWARD ISLAND, 4. SAINT JOHN, NEW BRUNSWICK,
5. LÉVIS, QUEBEC, 6. MONTREAL, QUEBEC, 7. OTTAWA, ONTARIO,
8. TORONTO, ONTARIO, 9. THUNDER BAY, ONTARIO, 10. WINNIPEG, MANITOBA,
11. REGINA, SASKATCHEWAN, 12. CALGARY, ALBERTA, 13. KAMLOOPS, BRITISH COLUMBIA,
14. PORT COQUITLAM, BRITISH COLUMBIA, 15. PORT RENFREW, BRITISH COLUMBIA

Terry trains even harder. Every day he runs. He never thinks about how far he has to go. He just takes one step at a time. To the corner. To the stop sign. To the tree.

Nothing will stop him from running. Not the flu. Not the blisters. Not his leg bleeding.

When I try to convince him to take a day off to rest his injuries, he gets mad. We argue. He keeps running.

A few months before the run, I start to have second thoughts. I'm supposed to drive the van, get Terry water and food, keep track of how far he runs each day, talk to reporters and collect money. *How will I do all of that? I can't talk to reporters. I don't know what to do if Terry gets hurt.* Again and again, I ask Terry to find someone else to go with him.

Soon, Terry loses patience with me. He stomps toward me. "You're my best friend. You have to go with me! Remember — take it one step at a time."

Terry looks so different now. Strong and powerful.

If Terry can do this, I can do this.

When spring arrives, Terry's ready. So am I.

We pick up the brand-new camper van that will be our home for the next five months. It has everything we need: Fridge. Stove. Stereo. Beds. Stinky chemical toilet.

We load the cupboards with all of Terry's favourite foods.
Cereal. Oranges. Chocolate chip cookies.
Canned spaghetti. Baked beans.
Peanut butter and jelly.

We gather all of Terry's running gear:
8 pairs of running shoes
5 white T-shirts
4 pairs of grey shorts
3 artificial legs
1 lucky sock

Our great adventure begins in a large city in Newfoundland where the island coastline meets the strong, rolling tides.

Side by side we stand on the rocky shore.

Terry dips his artificial leg into the swirling water. He turns to look up at the steep hill ahead.

"Just do your best, Terry." I smile.
"One step at a time."

Then he starts to run.

A NOTE FROM DARRELL FOX

My brother Terry accomplished the impossible. But as Terry always said, he didn't do it alone. I believe that if you look up the meaning of the word "friend," you should find Doug Alward's name. In 1980, Doug sacrificed and committed the whole year to supporting the Marathon of Hope — he was the only person by my brother's side every kilometre that he ran. Doug received no payment. His reward was supporting his best friend and witnessing him run into history while helping those less fortunate.

During the Marathon of Hope, everyone quickly recognized Terry's commitment, dedication and courage. To me, one of his finest traits was his humility. The same person who started the run was the same person who was forced to stop four and a half months later when cancer returned. When fame and fortune were offered at every turn, he quickly declined, asking instead for donations for cancer research. Doug matched Terry in this humility and has been practising and honing this trait now for 40 years. Doug always downplays his role. Terry needed a believer, someone who matched his never-give-up attitude and his stubbornness, who would be there through the good and not-so-good times. Thank you, Doug, for being Terry's friend.

"All my life I've been told I'm not
the biggest, the strongest,
or fastest or the smartest.
This is just one other challenge
for me to overcome."

— TERRY

From left: Darrell Fox, Terry Fox, Doug Alward,
Lévis, Quebec, during the Marathon of Hope, June 15, 1980
THE QUEBEC CHRONICLE-TELEGRAPH ARCHIVES /
SCOTT KINGSLAND

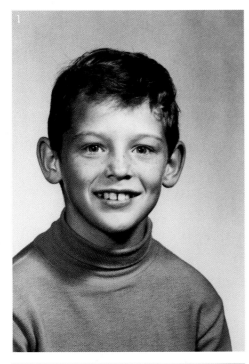

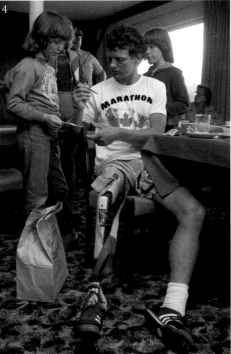

1. Terry in Grade 5

COURTESY THE FOX FAMILY

2. Mary Hill basketball team, 1972. Doug is #13; Terry is #15

COURTESY DOUG ALWARD

3. Terry wearing his beloved Darryl Sittler hockey jersey while speaking at Nathan Phillips Square, July 11, 1980

TORONTO GLOBE AND MAIL / JACK DOBSON

4. Terry signing autographs in Northern Ontario, August 13, 1980

TORONTO GLOBE AND MAIL / DENNIS ROBINSON

A NOTE FROM DOUG ALWARD

When an ordinary guy who is your best friend does something incredible, it doesn't seem like such a big deal. I had seen Terry do amazing things his whole life.

Terry always focused on what he could do with what he had. He set goals. And he worked hard to achieve those goals . . . When he was a C student or poorly skilled at sports, he studied or practised each day to get better. He hardly watched any TV and ate healthy vegetables and fruits. He listened to his parents' and teachers' suggestions. Eventually he became an A student and good at running, soccer, basketball and other activities.

After his right leg was 80% amputated, Terry said to me, "Thank God I have 20% of my leg left. The doctor left just enough thigh muscle for me to be able to swing the artificial leg so I can run." Most people would focus on the 80% of leg they had lost. Terry focused on what leg he had left and what was possible with it.

When Terry told me he wanted to run across Canada to raise money for cancer research, he asked me for advice. My first thought was, "I couldn't get you to run a 20-minute cross-country race in high school when you had two legs. How do you expect to run a 42-kilometre marathon every day on one leg?" But Terry was determined. He started running 100 metres a day, slowly adding a bit of distance until he was running 42 kilometres a day.

Forty years later, Terry still holds the world record for running on an artificial leg — 5373 kilometres in 143 days. Terry was just an ordinary guy who through hard work was able to do extraordinary things. As Terry always said, "One step at a time . . . "

COURTESY OF RITA IVANAUSKAS

TRAINING FOR THE MARATHON OF HOPE

My only training advice to Terry was to start with a little bit of running, maybe one lap of the track, and slowly add a bit every day. We figured it would take three years to work up to 42 kilometres a day. When Terry started, it was tough. But he wouldn't give up.

Terry was a real scientist. He kept careful records of his training. Here is an excerpt from his training journal:

Terry tried different foods to see what would give him energy for the run and wouldn't upset his stomach.

Monday, January 28, 1980

9:15 a.m. - Woke up; ate granola and toast

10:00 a.m. – Ran 24 kilometres; sunny day, very cold

1:30 p.m. – Lunch: four pieces of toast and Coke

2:30 p.m. – Ran 12 kilometres

Supper: fish, corn, potatoes, ice cream

6:45 p.m. – Weight training

Snack

9:00 p.m. – Wheelchair basketball

11:15 p.m. - Bed

Can you imagine that in freezing cold weather?

Terry ran 36 kilometres in training in a day. Incredible even on two legs!

Terry used weights to strengthen his back.

Terry played on the championship-winning team, the Cablecars, with Rick Hansen.

In just one year, Terry was ready to run across Canada! He could run a 42-kilometre marathon three hours faster than the amputee world record at that time. No wonder Terry was named Canada's Athlete of the Year and inducted into the Sports Hall of Fame!

TIMELINE

JULY 28, 1958

Terrance Stanley Fox is born in Winnipeg, Manitoba

1968

Terry and his family move to Port Coquitlam, British Columbia

1971

Grade 8, Mary Hill Junior High basketball tryout

1974

Terry and Doug start at Port Coquitlam High School

JUNE, 1976

Terry and Doug share the Athlete of the Year Award

SEPTEMBER, 1976

Terry and Doug begin studies at Simon Fraser University, Burnaby, British Columbia

MARCH 3, 1977

Terry learns he has cancer

MARCH 9, 1977

Terry's right leg is amputated

SUMMER, 1977

Terry begins playing wheelchair basketball

FEBRUARY, 1979

Terry begins training to run across Canada

SEPTEMBER, 1979

Terry and Doug run 28 km in the Prince George to Boston Race

APRIL 12, 1980

Terry and Doug begin the Marathon of Hope, St. John's, Newfoundland

SEPTEMBER 1, 1980

Terry ends his run outside of Thunder Bay, Ontario

JUNE 28, 1981

Terry dies. Public memorials are held across the country and the funeral is broadcast on national television

SEPTEMBER 13, 1981

The first Terry Fox Run is held, the beginning of what becomes an annual event

SEPTEMBER, 2020

The 40th anniversary of the Marathon of Hope. Three million kids participate in a Terry Fox School Run. More than 800 million dollars have been raised in Terry's name for cancer research

THE CANADIAN PRESS / BORIS SPREMO

"Even if I don't finish,
we need others to continue.
It's got to keep going without me."

— TERRY FOX